To Dorothy + Morris

As I glance through this book
I think of Max and Anna, Morris'
parents and Mama and Papa.

I am a child again and all
the things in the book are suddenly
very familiar, so commonplace

All my love
Harry

(Endel Markowitz)

KID-ISH YIDDISH

by
ENDEL MARKOWITZ

Illustrated by
DEBBY KLEIN

Haymark Publications, Inc.

Haymark Publications, Inc.
P.O. Box 243
Fredericksburg, VA 22404

Library of Congress Cataloging in Publication Data

ISBN 0-933910-05-3

Printed in **MEXICO**

FOR CHILDREN OF ALL AGES

The question is ... Is this book for children?

Well, if you were ever a child ...
If you are a child now ...
If you have a sense of humor ...
If you have a humorous sense ...

ENJOY ! ENJOY !

An explanation of Yiddish words appears at the end of the book.

KOSHER WISDOM

A *kosher* chicken found a hamster lying near a creek.
Said the chicken to the hamster, "My, you look so weak.
The problem is, you took a chance and didn't play it safe.
If only you were *kosher,* you wouldn't be so *trayf.*"

KISHKA AND KASHA

Kishka and *Kasha* are an unusual pair.
You can never find them at a country fair.
If you want to get them, you'll have to haunt,
a strictly *kosher* restaurant.

ANIMAL LOVERS

A *hoont* and a *ketzaleh* were sunning on a fence.
Dogs and cats are enemies, but to them it made no sense.
They both sat there together, as contented as could be
And watched the world go by them in stupid misery.

MR. MATZAH

When Mr. *Matzah* met Miss *Shmaltz*,
His heart went all aflutter,
And when they got together,
They were just like bread and butter.

CHOZZERAI

Mendle likes *kugle*.
Jake likes *borsht*.
Sammy likes *kreplach*,
Moisheh likes *voorsht*.

Yudle likes pizza,
Yussel likes pie.
Mix them all together,
And you've got *chozzerai*.

THE DREIDLE AND THE KISS

Sammy thought Sadie
was a beautiful *maidle*.
He went out and bought her
A colorful *dreidle*.

But to his dismay,
All went amiss.
What she really wanted
was a little kiss.

A YIDDISHEH MAMA

A *Yiddisheh mahmeh* will always say
That there's only one particular way
To knock out a cold and even the croup,
You've just got to drink her chicken soup.

LOX AND BAGELS

Lox and *bagels* ... *lox* and *bagels*,
Has more to it than Aesop's fables.
It's even better, if you please,
When you add a touch of rich cream cheese.

A CHANUKAH SLEIGH RIDE

Let's just suppose, on *Chanukah*,
To tell it like it is;
Chaim Cohen took Santa's sleigh
And claimed that it was his.

He hitched the reindeer,
pulled the reins,
And o'er the rooftops flew;
Yelling to the reindeer
Who knew what they must do ...

"On Berrel, Schmerrel, Yudle and Yussel ..."
Gay Moisheh, Yoisheh, Yahnkel and Russle ..."

From house to house they left the toys
For hundreds of sleeping girls and boys.
And when the night passed quickly by,
And the sun arose in the distant sky.

What Chaim said was just absurd;
This was exactly what we heard:

"OY VAY!"

MINNIE GOLDENBERG

Old Minnie Goldenberg, a *balibausteh* for sure,
Was beset with a terrible problem.
She had so many children and nothing to eat.
How would she feed them without any meat?

So she made chicken *shmaltz*,
Spread it on bread,
Then fed them and kissed them
And sent them to bed.

SHLAUG CAPOREHS

If you swing a chicken o'er your head,
You'll make quite sure the curse is dead.
For to rid yourself of all your *tzores*,
You only have to *shlaug caporehs*.

DELANCEY STREET

Delancey Street was jammed this day.
Pushcarts galore, in all array.
The merchandise was piled up high,
While people pushed and jostled by.

Everything in the world was there
From herring, to shoes, to underwear.
And as the crowd was milling around,
A strange kinship did there abound.

Kerchiefed women and bearded men
Spoke a language, known only to them.
An earthy tongue, that made them one;
A language born in a *pogrom*.

This was the Eastside, in old New York,
Where a spoon was a *leffil*, and a *gaupel*, a fork.
They loved this freedom; they had paid their dues.
These immigrant Americans, the Yiddish speaking Jews.

BOOK OF KNOWLEDGE

From the BOOK OF KNOWLEDGE
Let me quote
A most unusual anecdote:
"Though wealth and power
May be your wish;
It's not nearly as tasty
As *gefilteh* fish."

THE BATTLESHIP

A new Israeli battleship,
Cruising in the wind.
Named by a *Yiddisheh mahmeh*,
The *S.S. Mye Kiind*.

THE GAUGLE MAUGLE

When you're really sick, and your throat is sore,
And you've tried everything in the corner drug store.
You can heal yourself without a struggle;
Just use your *baubi's* cure, the *gaugle maugle*.

It was first concocted in a Russian *shtet'l*
Over an open fire in an iron kettle.
And though it may taste like a witch's brew,
It'll cure anything, from an ache to the flu.

A JEWISH VIGNETTE

When I was eight, and the world was new;
Life was simple and the days just flew.
We'd assemble in *chaydehr*, the kids in their place,
While the *rebbi* taught us the *alef, bayss*.

When I was thirteen, my parents were proud.
I recited the *kiddush*; my voice was so loud.
The *Bar Mitzvah* was great; and it was then
I received a gift, my first fountain pen.

When I was thirty, I took me a wife.
We lived and we loved; we had a good life.
A family we raised, three girls and a boy.
And as I look back, our life was a joy.

When I was sixty my hair turned to grey.
Our children were grown and went their own way.
We'd see them at times; but it wasn't the same.
Life is that way; there's no one to blame.

But now I am seventy, and as I recall
The blessings we had when the children were small,
I'm content in the fact that life is worth living;
It's a measure of taking and a measure of giving.

A MITZVAH

Life can offer many things.
It makes you happy with all it brings.
But the greatest joy of all, they say,
Is to perform a *mitzvah* on a given day.

The *Talmud* states, that your sacred mission
Is to help those in a needy position.
And so, you achieve your highest goal
With joy and gladness in your soul.

A *mitzvah* is charity, right from the heart,
Without selfish motives on anyone's part.
And when it occurs, your final reward
Is the joy of fulfilling the will of the Lord.

zaydeh

baubi

tahteh

zoon

tauchter

mahmeh

plimenik

ainikel

eyfele

plimenitzeh

fettehr

THE YIDDISH FAMILY TREE

BAUBI MYSEHS

Pas Kudnyak was nasty and mean.
The worst scoundrel you've ever seen.
He cheated old women and stole from his friends.
He would do anything to gain his ends.

Balma Locheh was a genius, they say.
He had the gift to make gold out of clay.
He once made a statue from pieces of wood;
And was given a medal, his work was so good.

Katchi Loppi was a messy old man.
He slept on the floor and ate from a can.
His clothing was wrinkled, his hair was wild.
He's been living like this since he was a child.

Pahv Aulyeh was careful and shy.
He never did things without knowing why.
Whenever he went to buy something new,
He held back the payment for a month or two.

Teddy *Trombenik* was spoiled and wild.
Truly a misfit since he was a child.
He'd tear his clothes and throw his shoe;
His parents were shocked at the things he'd do.

Baubi Myseh was a cute old girl.
Her ridiculous stories made your head whirl.
We all were aware her tales weren't true;
But she seemed so sincere, what else could we do?

Kuni Lemmehl was a sorry sight.
The problem was that he wasn't so bright.
He wanted to be like all the rest.
But the boy just couldn't pass the test.

Lahnger Luksh was skinny and tall.
Whenever he ran, we were sure he would fall.
He measured close to seven feet;
And his pants never failed to bulge at the seat.

STARRY NIGHT

Instead of a rainbow in the sky
That quickly fades as it goes by,
Wouldn't it be a wonderful sight
To see colored stars throughout the night?

THE CHAT

Mrs. *Nudnik* met Mrs. *Yenteh*
And so they stopped to chat.
"How old are your grandchildren now?"
Mrs. *Nudnik* always asked that.

Mrs. *Yenteh* didn't hesitate,
"The doctor is three and the lawyer is eight."

ITZIK YITZIK

Itzik Yitzik, the butcher's son,
Stole a *kishka* and away he run.
He stopped to eat, but was caught in a trap;
For he soon met up with the butcher's slap.

O'BRIEN'S DELI

Shelly and Nelly went into a deli
And ordered a corned beef on rye.
They both became flustered
When, instead of mustard,
They found there was butter inside.

A month later, or more,
They went back to the store,
And ordered the *matzah ball* soup.
They noticed a fly, in the bowl swimming by,
And they both were just thrown for a loop.

CHUTZPA

Chutzpa is a lot of things, rolled up into one.
Chuztpa is the thing you need, if you want to get things done.
It stops your knees from shaking; it raises up your chin,
If you have to face a problem that you'd rather not be in.

It can get you out of trouble, if you make a bad mistake.
It will change someone's opinion, if you're known to be a fake.
Your chest will stick out proudly; your voice will echo loud,
If you happen to be facing an unruly, hostile crowd.

You can build a mighty fortune; you can mingle with a king.
The power is within you, though you started on a string.
The thing you need is *chutzpa*, and the power it can give,
To the one who knows its secret on the only way to live.

FARMISHT   FARTUMELT

Mr. and Mrs. Goldblatt went out for
the evening and left their baby in
Baubi Goldblatt's care. *Baubi* decided
to bake a cake while the baby was
sleeping. When the cake had fully
risen, she opened the oven door
and began to take the cake out of the
oven.

Suddenly, the doorbell and the telephone
began to ring, loudly; both at the same time!

FARBLUNDJET   FARPOTCHKET

Baubi Goldblatt froze in horror.
If she pushed the cake back into the
oven and closed the door, the cake
would fall.

Now she was *farmisht*.

If she let the doorbell ring, the baby would wake up.

She became *fartumelt*.

If she ran to the door, the phone would continue to ring.

By this time, she was completely *farblundjet*.

And the entire situation became *farpotchket*.

PICKLES AND LIMES

If a lime costs a nickle
And a pickle costs a dime.
It really is confusing
To buy them all the time.

Because pickle rhymes with nickle
And lime rhymes with dime,
You'd be paying a nickle for a pickle
And a dime for a lime.

YOU CAN BANK ON IT!

Here You Have a Friend.　　　Here You Have Security　　　But Here You Have *Mishpocheh!*

MISCHA MISHUGENER

Was born on *mauntik*.

His *bris* was on *dinstik*.

He was married on *mitvauch*.

He took sick on *daunehrshtik*.

He became worse on *frytik*.

He was a bar mitzvah on *Shabbas*.

He was buried on *zoontik*.

And that is the *geshichti* of
Misha Mishugener.

SHABBAS

Shabbas comes on Friday night;
And a prayer is heard in the candlelight.
As mama, with covering on her head,
Blesses the *challah*, the braided egg bread.

The children listen in solemn awe,
Though they've seen this many times before.
And in their hearts comes a silent pledge
To never forget their heritage.

EXPLANATION OF YIDDISH WORDS

ainikel	grandchild
alef	first letter of the Hebrew alphabet
auranzsh	orange
bagel	doughnut-shaped roll
balibausteh	a proficient homemaker
balmalocheh	a capable person
bar mitzvah	a religious ceremony celebrated by a boy of thirteen
baubi	grandmother
baubi myseh	fairy tale
bayss	second letter of the Hebrew alphabet
bloy	blue
borsht	beet soup
bris	rite of circumcision
broyn	brown
challah	braided loaf of egg bread
Chanukah	Festival of Lights
chaydehr	Hebrew school
chozzerai	junk food
chutzpa	brazen nerve
daunehrshtik	Thursday
dinstik	Tuesday
dreidle	four-sided spinning top
eyfele	baby
farblundjet	confused
farmisht	mixed up
fartumelt	stunned
farpotchket	all messed up
faygel	bird
fettehr	uncle
frytik	Friday
gaugle maugle	an old Jewish cure-all
gaupil	fork
gay / gayt	go / goes

gefilteh fish	chopped fish balls
gehshichti	story
gel	gold
goulash	a meat and vegetable dish
grin	green
groy	grey
hoont	dog
kasha	buckwheat groats
katchiloppi	a messy person
ketzaleh	kitten
kishka	A Jewish food similar to sausage
kiddush	blessing over wine
kugle	a potato or noodle pudding
kosher	fit to eat according to Jewish dietary laws
kreplach	meat filled dumplings
kunilemmehl	a foolish person
lahngerluksh	a tall, slim person
leffil	spoon
lox	smoked salmon
mahmeh	mother
maidle	young girl
matzah	unleavened bread
matzah ball	matzah meal dumpling
mauntik	Monday
misha	ugly
mishpocheh	relatives
mishugener	a crazy person
mitzvah	a good deed
mitvauch	Wednesday
nudnik	an annoying person
oy vay	an expression of resignation
pahvaulyeh	to be careful
paskudnyak	a nasty person
plemenik	nephew
plimenitzeh	niece

pogrom	a persecution
rebbi	rabbi
royt	red
Shabbos	Sabbath
shlaug caporehs	an old Jewish superstition
shmaltz	rendered chicken fat
shtet'l	a Jewish village in Europe
S. (ess) S. (ess) mye kiind	eat, eat, my child
tahteh	father
Talmud	Jewish laws and commentary
tauchter	daughter
trayf	non-kosher
trombenik	a troublesome person
tzores	troubles
veis	white
voorsht	salami
Yiddisheh mahmeh	Jewish mother
yenteh	busybody
zaydeh	grandfather
zoon	son
zoontik	Sunday

YIDDISH NAMES
Berrel
Chaim
Itzik
Mendle
Moisheh
Russle
Schmerrel
Yahnkel
Yitzik
Yoisheh
Yudle
Yussel